COCKROACH
曱甴

Also by Ho Ka Kei (Jeff Ho)

Iphigenia and the Furies (On Taurian Land) & Antigone: 方 trace

COCKROACH
曱甴

HO KA KEI
(JEFF HO)

Playwrights Canada Press
Toronto

First edition: June 2024
Printed and bound in Canada by Imprimerie Gauvin Ltée, Gatineau

Jacket art and design by Jeremy Leung
Author photo by Dahlia Katz

Playwrights Canada Press
202-269 Richmond St. W., Toronto, ON M5V 1X1
416.703.0013 | info@playwrightscanada.com | www.playwrightscanada.com

For professional or amateur production rights, please contact:
Sean Miller, Gary Goddard Agency
250 The Esplanade, Suite 304, Toronto, ON M5A 1J2
416-928-0299 | sean@ggagency.ca

LIBRARY AND ARCHIVES CANADA CATALOGUING IN PUBLICATION
Title: Cockroach = Ga zhat / Ho Ka Kei (Jeff Ho).
Other titles: Ga zhat
Names: Ho, Jeff, author.
Description: Chinese characters in title transliterated.
| Text in English, with some text in Chinese.
Identifiers: Canadiana (print) 20240370848 | Canadiana (ebook) 20240375092
| ISBN 9780369104953 (softcover) | ISBN 9780369104977 (EPUB)
| ISBN 9780369104960 (PDF)
Subjects: LCGFT: Drama.
Classification: LCC PS8615.O155 C63 2024 | DDC C812/.6—dc23

Playwrights Canada Press staff work across Turtle Island, on Treaty 7, Treaty 13, and Treaty 20 territories, which are the current and ancestral homes of the Anishinaabe Nations (Ojibwe / Chippewa, Odawa, Potawatomi, Algonquin, Saulteaux, Nipissing, and Mississauga / Michi Saagiig), the Blackfoot Confederacy (Kainai, Piikani, and Siksika), néhiyaw, Sioux, Stoney Nakoda, Tsuut'ina, Wendat, and members of the Haudenosaunee Confederacy (Mohawk, Oneida, Onondaga, Cayuga, Seneca, and Tuscarora), as well as Metis and Inuit peoples. It always was and always will be Indigenous land.

We acknowledge the financial support of the Canada Council for the Arts, the Ontario Arts Council (OAC), Ontario Creates, the Government of Ontario, and the Government of Canada for our publishing activities.

Canada Council for the Arts | Conseil des arts du Canada
ONTARIO ARTS COUNCIL
CONSEIL DES ARTS DE L'ONTARIO
an Ontario government agency
un organisme du gouvernement de l'Ontario
ONTARIO CREATES | ONTARIO CRÉATIF
Canada
Ontario

For Pierre.

foreword

Hanna Kiel

Before I had the pleasure of meeting Jeff, I had the opportunity to delve into his remarkable play *cockroach (甲由)*. The invitation to collaborate as a choreographer for this captivating production opened up a world of fascination for me. As a Korean Canadian artist I was immediately drawn to Jeff's storytelling and his portrayal of the intricate character at the core of this narrative. Remarkably, our initial encounter took place via Zoom, yet, even through the digital realm, I could sense the warmth of his generosity and his openness.

cockroach (甲由) marked my inaugural venture as a contemporary choreographer, and I found an instant connection with Jeff's unique approach to storytelling. His writing in this play transcends the mere exploration of a boy's trauma; it delves into the profound notion that our entire lives can be entangled with a singular event. It's a journey of retrospection and the process of learning to coexist with an indescribable painbody.

What struck me most about Jeff's work is the way he crafted this play. It is a narrative battleground where two languages and cultures clash and intertwine. Through a blend of humour and anger, direct and indirect approaches, concealment and revelation, Jeff masterfully navigates the complex themes of immigrant life, queer experiences, racism, and the quest for identity. The question of how to talk about these subjects looms large: Is there an appropriate way to speak of these things, or does such a way even exist? It's within the play's dialogues that we find the clues and answers that guide us through the odyssey of this painbody. The language within the play has a way of deceiving, unsettling, confronting, and entertaining, leading us to an eventual reckoning with the boy at the centre of it all.

What I cherish most about *cockroach (甲由)* is that it propels us on an unpredictable journey. It's a ride that we can't control or predict, and we're left uncertain about the final destination, which adds to the intrigue.

My collaboration with Jeff on his brilliant play, and our exploration of the depths of painbody memories, has left an indelible mark on me. I've emerged from this experience as a transformed artist. *cockroach (甲由)* has been a profound catalyst in reshaping my creative path, and for that, I'm profoundly grateful.

Dora Mavor Moore Award–winner Hanna Kiel is from Seoul, South Korea, and moved to Vancouver, Canada, in 1996. She has presented her work at 12 Minutes Max, PlanB Singles and Solos Festival, and the Dancing on the Edge Festival in Vancouver. In 2007, she collaborated with Yoko Ono as a dancer and choreographer at the Centre A. Moving to Toronto in 2008, Hanna has continued choreographing for Rosedale Heights School of the Arts, Conteur Dance Academy, George Brown Dance, Ryerson Dances, School of Toronto Dance Theatre, ProArteDanza, Jörgen Dance, the National Ballet of Canada, Canadian Contemporary Dance Theatre, Toronto Dance Theatre, Dusk Dances, Tarragon Theatre, Silk Bath Collective, and Decidedly Jazz Danceworks in Calgary. In 2012 she won Northwest Dance Project's Pretty Creatives international choreographic competition, and she was an e-choreographer in 2015 for Springboard Danse Montreal. Hanna is the artistic director of Human Body Expression Dance Company.

foreword

Mike Payette

What is particularly inspiring about new creation in Canada is the capacity to layer in the intersections of cultural identity that make this land mutually vibrant and unique. The storytellers and caretakers that have protected our collective opportunity to find freedom in this country—therefore adding to the breadth of how individual stories can be shared—offer powerful bridges for those of us who have been brought here or have found a comfort in being able to thrive.

When I was appointed as Tarragon's artistic director in 2021, we sought to expand our focus on what it means to be a playwright, and what it means to be Canadian today. In this investigation, the tie back continues to swim toward the notion of "intersectionality"; yes, from a cultural perspective, but also from how those dynamics lend themselves to artistic form and the range in which unique experiences can reach universal and heightened theatricality.

Jeff Ho's text is enrobed with the very collisions that represent so many that have called this country home. His connectivity to language assimilation and the pursuit of individuality balanced by the throes of otherdom within a once-connected homeland of Hong Kong vibrates off the page. His skill in marrying prose and profound imagery is supported by the simplicity of one boy navigating a traumatic event that humanizes him beyond the complexities of "who am I" and reminds us of the many vulnerabilities so many occupy. One can simply ride the wave reading *cockroach (曱甴)* and feel inspired, gutted, isolated, and hopeful all in the same held breath.

The world we created in our production was responsive to Jeff's ask of the text, as if he himself was embodying the Bard, desiring us to listen to it, respect it, and to be free to interpret it. Like the classical musician he is, Jeff expertly allows us to lean into the text's musicality—and like any rich text—imagine the theatrical backdrop these three souls cohabitate. Working with celebrated choreographer Hanna Kiel, we built a framework that engaged the body in this heightened world, shining light on the image when the spoken word wasn't enough. In this case, surely the text defines this world, and the body offers a synchronistic language that elevates the inherent danger of this tale.

This connection to danger is the undertone of *cockroach (曱甴)*. It rumbles through the pages and in the conditions from which Jeff is inspired—the danger of being from a land that is consciously othering, or the danger of seeking refuge in unknown territory amalgamated with the perils of coming-of-age and the crossroads of learning how to acclimate to new surroundings and new personal discoveries. Certainly, the act of living is a war in and of itself (not unlike riding the streetcars of the TTC) and *cockroach (曱甴)* is Jeff's sword.

Jeff's mastery in evoking conflict in humanity is deeply rewarded by urging us to see ourselves in the Cockroach, the Bard, and altogether the Boy's journey, and with him take a moment to envision a lifted horizon.

A question lingers as the Boy's snapshot reliving unravels: Will he make it? The pursuit of going through the trenches of this cataclysmic moment is ultimately to survive, not to remedy. Through the Boy's multiplicities, he uncovers a new language that is unique to his ability to take one step beyond the trauma. To breathe into the chaos and grow from it. As audience members we inhale with Cockroach's first toke of catnip and collectively exhale with the invitation for the Boy to dream.

I believe he does.

Mike Payette is a director, educator, and actor who has appeared at some of Canada's finest theatres. He has worked with incredible companies across the country including the Citadel, Vertigo, Banff Centre, Geordie, Artistic Fraud of Newfoundland, Repercussion Theatre, Segal Centre, Centaur, the Grand, Factory Theatre, Neptune, and the National Arts Centre, among others. Directing credits include Come Home: The Legend of Daddy Hall, cockroach (甲由), Paint Me This House of Love *(Tarragon),* Blithe Spirit *(Shaw Festival),* Choir Boy *(Canadian Stage/Arts Club Theatre),* Harlem Duet *(Black Theatre Workshop),* Another Home Invasion *(Tableau D'Hôte Theatre),* Hosanna *and* Choir Boy *(Centaur),* Around the World in 80 Days, Virginia Wolf, The Paperbag Princess, *and* Reaching for Starlight *(Geordie),* Venus, Burning Vision, *and* Indecent *(National Theatre School),* Sensitivity *(Obsidian Theatre/CBC Gem), the Quebec premiere of* Héritage—A Raisin in the Sun *(Théâtre Duceppe), along with the national tours of* The Tashme Project *(Tashme Prod/Centaur/Factory/Firehall), and Lorena Gale's* Angélique *(BTW/Tableau D'Hôte/NAC/Factory/Obsidian). Mike is a two-time Montreal English Theatre Award (META) recipient and was the co-founding artistic director of Tableau D'Hôte Theatre and past assistant artistic director for Black Theatre Workshop. He was also artistic and executive director of Geordie Productions in Montreal before becoming artistic director of Tarragon Theatre in Toronto, where he is currently based.*

cockroach (甲甴) was first produced by Tarragon Theatre in their Mainspace, Toronto, from September 13 to October 9, 2022, with the following cast and creative team:

Bard: Karl Ang
Cockroach: 郝邦宇 Steven Hao
Boy: Anton Ling

Director: Mike Payette
Choreographer: Hanna Kiel
Set and Costume Design: Christine Ting-Huan 挺歡 Urquhart
Lighting Design: Arun Srinivasan
Sound Design and Original Score: Deanna H. Choi
Associate Director: Damon Bradley Jang
Production Dramaturgy: Myekah Payne
Assistant Sound Design: River Cecil Oliveira
Sound Design Intern: Tristan Chung
Stage Manager: Emilie Aubin
Apprentice Stage Manager: Jaimee Q. Vicente-Hall

characters

Cockroach
Bard
Boy

notes

Chapter 1: "Ooo Sac" is pronounced "ouuu" like in "you."

Chapter 2: The GASPS are to be spoken out loud.
The brb's wtf's lol's . . . each letter must be spoken out loud.

punctuation notes

A forward slash (/) is an interruption
A *beat* is a one count of silence
A *pause* is a three-to-five count of silence

When there are punctuation marks, they indicate a sense of music. When there are a lack of punctuation marks, it indicates a legato drive through the line.

casting notes

When casting for this play, please take diligence and care in reflecting the conversations around Hong Kong politics, Queer Chinese identity, and trauma within your own communities. Cockroach and the Boy ideally should be Cantonese speakers (Mandarin is okay for the cockroach), while the Bard may be cast from IBPOC communities that reflect or neighbour the themes of this play.

chapter 1—intrusion

Something so horrific,
A passing,
A disaster,
An assault,
Is happening.
In moments of horror
We search for a word,
A distance,
A role to play,
To withstand the bleak.

We see a boy.
He seems to be muttering something
Over and over again.

BOY
(under his breath) Be to be to be to be to be to be to be to be to be to
Be to be to be to be to be to be to be to be to be to

Trauma forces people to splinter
Apart from themselves,
Doesn't it?

We see one of these splinters (the BARD) hover above the boy
But they do not speak.

We see another splinter,
COCKROACH,
Crawl from some abyss,
Down down down, coming up.

It takes time to even feel that you've splintered, doesn't it?

Sometimes, these splinters speak on our behalf,
They must speak on our behalf,
And so
COCKROACH joins in.

BOY
(under his breath) Be to be to be to be to be to be to be to be to be to
Be to be to be to be to be to be to be to be to be to

COCKROACH
(simultaneously with the BOY) To be to be to be to be to be to be to be to be to be to be
To be to be to be to be to be to be to be to be to be

COCKROACH intrudes,
Takes over.

The BOY and the BARD
Do not disappear,
But they seem to fade in some way.

COCKROACH gets up on stage.
It's gotta be magic, but also not,
Cuz that's just how roaches are anyway.

They look out at the audience,
Gauge the room,
Light up a joint.

COCKROACH
To be
To be
To be

Beat.

A cockroach smoking a roach,
Can you imagine that?

Well that's what I am,
Whatchu gonna do 'bout it?

Ain't smoking weed though, that shit's legal now,
But hella expensive.

I'm smoking catnip.
Watchu gonna do 'bout that?

Catnip ain't just for cats.
Unlike those feline failures,
You won't see me rolling around,
Whiskers ablaze,
Meowing like some fur zombie.

Catnip just makes me chill.
And I need some chill right now.

Here, want some?

COCKROACH offers a hit of catnip to the audience.
Someone in the audience may cough,
As they always do when there's a fog machine
Or any semblance of smoke or impurity in the air.

(if someone coughs) Watchu coughing about?
The catnip smoke burning your
Homo sapien lungs?

Truss me,
That ain't the only thing that's gonna give you a cough.

(if no one coughs, COCKROACH will) Oh my oh my,
That shit hits hard.
Oof, my li'l roach lungs can't compare to you
Humans.

But truss.
I'll give you something to cough about one way or another.

I eat your food,
I eat your skin,
Sometimes I gnaw on your eyebrows,
Eyelashes,
Dandruff,
Nails,
What have you.

Nutritious? Maybe not,
But sure as hell tasty.

But don't worry,
I won't bite.
Promise.

I feel like we got off to a wrong start,
Gotta introduce, that's how y'all humans do it, yea?
Gotta introduce myself to each and every one of you.

COCKROACH steps on the blunt of catnip.
It sizzles and fades.

Welcome.

You can call me Blatta.
Hate the name, don't call me that.
You can call me cockroach, or roach for short.
Blatta's my legal name.

Mama Blatta shat me outta her ooo sac.
I made that up, it's not actually called ooo sac,
It's oothecae,
But that shit's too fancy to say,
So I just say ooo sac.
Anyway, Mama Blatta, ooo sac, twelve siblings,
All dead, just me left,
All alone,
No mama to be seen,
No papa to be mentioned,
No siblings to be cannibalized,
Just me, alone,
Finding my way through this dark dark world.
Well not actually that dark,
Cuz Hong Kong, you know Hong Kong?
City of Lights.
No, I'm not talking about Paris,
Cuz that name ain't true,
Paris dank as hell.
I'm talking about HONG KONG,
True city of lights,
Never dark,
Neon pink,
Ever limo green banners,
Crimson-red symbols
From dusk till dawn till dusk.
HONG FUCKING KONG.

Or as I like to call it.
Tian Tang (天國)
Paradise.
Paradisio.

Everything a li'l roach could wish for,
Damp, humid, stormy weather,
Perfect temperature,
Plenty of sewers to spa out in,
Plenty of food stalls to prey on,
Plenty of plenty.
But deeply problematic,
Ya know, cuz Blatta.
Remember, I hate that name,
But a name is a name,
A blatta is a blatta,
And you know what it means?

The insect that shuns the light.

Yea. Me. Blatta.
Shunning light,
In the city of lights.
HA.

A name that doesn't fit seems fitting
For a li'l roach like me,
Cuz I don't fit nowhere,
Never have never will.

Mama Blatta
Conceived me and my twelve siblings back in . . .
Guess.
Seriously, you'll never get this.
Guess.
HOUSTON, WE'VE GOT A PROBLEM.
Yea. Of all places.

The great red, white, and blue,
Weird to admit,
Cuz Americans get a bad rap,
But blood is blood.
I'm an American Cockroach, naturalized Hong Kong citizen.
Don't tell China though,
They'd extradite me.
HA.

Mama Blatta met Papa Blatta
At a Whitney Houston concert,
June 2, 1991.
It's true,
It happened.
DON'T google it.

They were munching on Whitney's wigs,
Making love,
While she was, "I WILL ALWAYS LOVE youuuUUUu,"
And Papa Blatta, bless his spirit,
Got blasted outta the wig when Whitney swung her head
And got trampled on by a bodyguard.
Mama Blatta was left all alone, with a full ooo sac,
Trapped in Whitney's wig.

That very wig got a real clean,
But Mama Blatta was strong,
Cockroach does what cockroach must,
Survive hairspray,
Survive the dry-clean tumble,
Survive it all.

The wig, along with Mama Blatta,
Got packed up, vacuum-sealed,
And sent to the airport.

You better believe cockroaches fly,
Cuz wherever you go,
Whatever you pack,
There we be.

I mean, hell,
Ya know my cuz went to space, right?

I'm serious,
My cuz, Nadezhda,
She was sent into space by the Russians.
She flew up into space a hot young thang
And came back down to earth a grandma.
First thing from earth ever to give birth in space.

We'll multiply and explode in numbers to match the stars,
Cuz wherever you go,
There we be.

Anyway,
Mama Blatta finally wiggled her way outta Whitney's wigs,
Lifted her spiky legs, and pierced a hole through the vacuum-sealed plastic wrap
And ran, like no cockroach has ran before.
She zigzagged through the airport,
Took a moment to snack on a doughnut or two,
Didn't even realize it'd be her last Boston cream she'd ever get to taste,
Made a pit stop at the gent's room and took a quick nap in the urinal,
And kept running, heaving and sighing,
Ooo sac trembling up and down,
The weight of thirteen baby roaches weighing on her spiky legs.

Then—her antennae rose. AHA!
She felt that . . . how do you say it in the West,
A calling, fate, destiny, a clarion call,
A that is that.

And she found herself in this . . .
Black-haired, black-eyed baby's diaper.
She didn't know what to call them back then.
Mama Blatta had no sense of what human was of what background.
I mean,
No offence,
YOU ALL LOOK THE SAME TO US.
But that Chinese baby's diaper
Was a haven.

Beat.

Landed here, City of Lights.

Mama Blatta was stuck, trapped between the baby's chunky thighs
That you just wanna take a bite out of.
I gotta admit,
Human babies are SO cute.
I mean, you should have seen me as a baby.
I looked like a grain of rice, except with hairy legs.

Mama Blatta travelled with this Chinese family,
To their home,
In Kwok Lai Tzo,
And immediately felt a kinship with them in this new city.

But that's when tragedy struck.

You see, Mama did not know the ritual of humans,
That diapers are not permanent sanctuaries,
That they are disposable,
Like life, I suppose, one use only.

And as the parents chucked the diaper out the bin,
Mama was caught with it.
Mama was trapped between a cigarette butt and a literal piece of shit
that was stuck on the butt part of the diaper.

She tried and tried and fought and fought.
Yet.
Mama Blatta was no match for the walls of a garbage bag.

With the remaining strength in her body,
Mama Blatta lifted her spiky legs,
Looked up at the closing plastic above her,
And yelled out:

BARD
(as Mama Blatta) Hssssssssssssssssssssssssssssssss—

COCKROACH
"I GOT OUTTA WHITNEY'S WIG,
THIS BAG WILL NOT BE THE END OF—"

She never got to finish that sentence.
For you see,
The humans gave the bag a squeeze,
Tried to fit it into the chute,
And it crushed . . .
It . . . ended Mama.

With her dangling spiky leg,
And from the sheer power of fate, and the precise angle where plastic
Met leg—it pierced the tiniest of holes,
Just enough for her tumbling ooo sac to free itself from the chute,
And stick itself onto a wall.

And so there we were.
Twelve siblings unborn,
But already a life lived,
Cuz that's how it goes with us roaches.
We know everything that ever happened to our ancestors.
Everything.
It's a tiresome thing to hold so many lives in our tiny little brains.

But even, my great-great-great-great-great-great-great-great-great-great—okay,
It's far too many greats to list,
But my greatest of grandmas has been stuck in a piece of amber for over
Fifty million years.
And I remember just how she got stuck,
Trying to suckle maple outta a darn tree.

And we evolve,
Cuz we remember everything that's ever happened in our family.
We evolve faster than you can blink.
All y'all thought you were so smart when you developed sugar traps to bait us.
JOKE'S ON YOU.
Less than a generation later,
We developed a glucose aversion,
Like, literally, sugar isn't sweet to us no more.
What was once sweet, now bitter.

And so we find ways around your traps,
Back into the darkness of your homes.

My siblings, bless them,
All twelve of them, power-washed from the walls where the ooo sac stuck.

But me?
My placement in the sac,
Just ever so slightly off, perfect accident,
Propelling me on a water slide through the pipes,
Through the sewers,
Through the filtering system,
Through your filth,
Through your chemicals,
Through your condos,

Through your sink,
And right back into your home.

Go home.
Go home.
Go home.

No matter how far life has thrown me,
I end up here,
Next to this Chinese baby.
Y'all are WEIRD.
I grew up in a week,
Took this baby years to even learn how to feed itself.
Taught myself how to survive
The instant I got outta that ooo sac,
Yet your babies whimper and wail like weak papayas flopping about.

And what do you do for that baby?
You coddle it,
Baby-talk at it,
Ooh ooh aah aah at its face,
Kiss its sweet cheek,
Pinch its tubey thighs.
And what?

You feed it,
You read to it,
You watch as hair and teeth appear,
You raise the baby with love and patience,
Withstand the thousand-decibel cries,
Change its diapers,
Wheel them around in strollers.

And one day they start blubbering,
Start making sounds,
Form words
That make your hearts feel some sort of bubble-wrapped warmth,

Make you feel closer to them.
And they grow up with those forming words,
Modelling themselves after the ones who raise them.
They sponge it all up,
How you wake up
How you stretch
How you breathe
How you shit
How you clean
How you brush your teeth
How you comb your hair
How you dress yourself
How you dance
How you laugh
How you love
How you resist
How you embrace
How you empathize
How you rebel
How you care
How you hate
How you treat others
How you greet neighbours
How you yell at others
How you demonize others
How you dehumanize others
How you other others.

And they inherit it all,
Your babies.
They inherit you.
Your culture, your traditions, your governments,
Your laws, your logic, your unreasonable expectation.

The sound of a terrifying burp.

This Chinese baby boy certainly did.

How did you all learn to shit so hard on yourselves?
Did you inherit that too?

Yet, somehow,
You've also inherited our identity as insult.
You wield our name as a curse.
You throw
"YOU'RE A COCKROACH"
At anything you want to get rid of.

You scream
"DIE, COCKROACH"
At other humans you wish to see extinct.

The Germans have done it.
The Hutus.
The Chinese.
Even now,
NOW, and in the future,
You label each other as cockroaches,
To what?
Reduce your enemy's humanity?
Strip them of the fact that they too
Once were babies
That babbled the same sounds as you,
That were coddled like you,
That saw the world through their parents' eyes.
Humans raising humans, exterminating humans.

You loathe that which you foster.

How amusing.
And frankly,
What the fuck, peeps.
Choose another insect to curse with.
Why not a fucking fly, or a wasp,

Or those useless butterflies that do nothing
But dress up and drift towards the sun?

Why do you do this?
I gotta say,
Seems to me from womb to baby to adult to old geezer,
The one thing you've inherited amongst yourselves
Is
Fear.

What are you scared of?
What makes you fight or flight?
What makes your skin crawl and your heart squeeze?

Why?
And what is your fear
Of anything other,
Of anything that
Feels like . . . like a cockroach in your mind?

There's a word for it.
I eat dictionaries for dessert,
So I know what the fuck I'm talking about:

Katsaridaphobia.

Fear of cockroaches.

Are you scared of me?

The BBC wrote about it.
Yes, I eat magazines too,
Eating is my way of reading, all right?
Has the BBC written about you?
No?
Then don't question me and listen up, fool.

They wrote that we, cockroaches,
Are the source of a great many nightmares.

So much so that there are therapies to fix katsaridaphobia,
VR treatments,
Where scientists program pixellated versions of my beautiful self,
Where you can be in virtual space with virtual roaches.

I mean, don't go wasting thousands of dollars trying to get a feel for me,
I'm standing here, right in front of you,
Carapace and all.
You can touch me,
It's okay,
Feel me up,
I don't care.
I'm not scared.

But your brains,
They're elastic.
They store new information to replace the old.
You have therapy to condition fear out of you,
To desensitize, normalize, neutralize
That scaredy cat in your brain.
So that you can be numb from what would make you leap.

But fear branches, doesn't it?
One thing grows into the next.
You conquer your fear of roaches
And something else takes its place.
Sometimes it becomes literal.

This researcher dude, this scientist,
Who I hate.
I mean, I don't hate much,
But this dude,

He literally held a prison of thousands of my family members in his lab,
Ripping off spikey legs,
Antennae,
Chopping off our heads,
To figure out what we were.

William Bell, google that.
Famous cockroach dude.
He studied us for so long,
Poked things into our shit for so long,
That he ended up allergic to our poop,
Like literally.
He studied us so hard
That he became allergic to us
And became unable to eat our distant cousins, the lobsters.

KARMA. BILL BELL.

Besides, lobsters.
Who you call roaches of the sea.
As if it's some insult, some tarnish.
If only you knew the the the
Sheer beauty, that sapphire glow of their shells,
Those bulging, dark, onyx eyes,
Those pincers,
Like holdmedown and takemenow, amirite?

I . . . I had a chance once.
To be loved by and
To have loved a lobster.

Rosie.
My sweet.

My love at first sight, rockets exploding in my brain,
My heart singing, angels trumpeting, thunder clouds colliding
Love.

I was taking a walk one day,
Just a casual roachy jaunt down the street,
A venture out from
Baby boy's abode.
I pass by this restaurant,
And there they were.
Behind this glass pane,
Trapped in their own li'l aquarium,
Their own li'l prison.
Rosie,
All alone.
Tapping tapping tapping at the glass,
Which I took to be their way of saying,
"HELP ME SAVE ME RELEASE ME."

BOY
(simultaneously with "HELP ME SAVE ME RELEASE ME") No more.
Please.
Let me go.

Beat.

COCKROACH
And my heart stopped,
Almost quite literally as a taxi nearly stomps me dead.
But no,
Because I . . .
I don't think I've ever seen a shell as stunning as their's.
Just . . . the look of them, and the vibrancy of their their being,
And I gasped.

I roached my way over,
Crawled up on the slippery glass,
And peered right through.

Tap tap tap tap tap tap.
Tap tap.
Tap.

Rosie said.

And.
I had no idea what the fuck they were saying.
I don't speak lobster.
So I yell back.

"I HAVE NO IDEA WHAT THE FUCK YOU'RE SAYING."

Rosie responds.

Tap.
Tap tap.
Tap.
TAP TAP.

Beat.

"WHAT?"

Beat.

TAPPITY TAPPITY TAP

Beat.

"You want . . . out?"

Beat.

TAP!

Beat.

"I'll . . . I'll see what I can do, be right back.
Oh.
I'm . . . I'm.
You can call me cockroach."

Beat.

TAP TAP TAAAAAAAAP.

Beat.

And I scurried off,
Looking for an entrance to this glass thing,
And I looked for holes, for gaps, for a string to pull Rosie out from,
Or a vacuum to suck them out,
I dunno,
Anything.
I was desperate.

And I searched and searched
And I found this net, and I thought,
Rosie can cling on, and I can drag them out,
And then I'll lug them down by the water,
And that's that,
Freedom for Rosie,
And then we'll meet every night, and then eventually
I'll find a sewer close by, and I can live there, and they can live with me,
Right in the water,
And I can make a ring out of braided cat hair and tape it together with baby boy's diapers,

And propose,
And get married,
And somehow we'll have cockroach–lobster hybrid babies,
And we'll have a happy happy family.
And I'll never leave them like Mama Blatta did us,
Cuz we'll be safe in the sewer,
And I'll advise my cockroach–lobster babies to avoid wigs,
And vacuums,
And show them the ropes,
And tell them the funny story of how I saved Rosie with a net,
And then I'll die with Rosie by my side,
And they'll die later cuz lobsters have longer lives,
And then we'll live on and on through the beautiful memories
Of our beautiful children.

So, I lug my net on my shoulders,
And I make my way back to Rosie.
And.
I climb up the glass thing.

And they were gone.

Beat.

I look over at this group of humans,
And they're laughing and clanging chopsticks and teacups,
And they point inside this bowl.
I climb up a wall for a better view.
And . . .
Unmistakably.
Rosie.
Their tomato shell split apart, swimming in a soup.
Rosie's skull,
Still intact, like treasure, resting at the lip of the bowl.
I let go of my net.
It falls on a grandma
And she shrieks,

"AI YA."
But I don't care.
I turn away.
I can no longer watch as these humans and their clanging chopsticks and teacups
Take another bite outta . . . outta . . .

Pause.

You. Humans. Monsters.
How dare you eat us all?
How dare you nickname us and pit us against one another.
Roaches of the sea?

What is that?
What is that fear of the other?
What is your motive behind it?

Why?

Like it's a travesty.
A murder of crows.
(Terrifying.)
A school of fish.
(Bitch, those things don't learn nothing, no amount of school can fix that.)
A shrewdness of apes.
(Have you seen them? They ain't shrewd!)
A swarm of bees.
Okay, I'll give you that one, that one feels accurate.
A family of beavers.
(AWWWW. They're so cute.)
A caravan of camels.
A destruction of wildcats.
A cauldron of bats.
A coalition of cheetahs.
A parade of elephants.

A tower of giraffes.
A thunder of hippopotamuses.
A cackle of hyenas.
An embarrassment of pandas.
An aurora of polar bears.
A harem of seals.
A wisdom of wombats.
A labour of moles.
A conspiracy of lemurs.
A blessing of narwhals.
A dazzle of zebras.
A convocation of eagles.
A kettle of hawks.
A parliament of owls.
An unkindness of ravens.
A tuxedo of penguins.
A slaughter of iguanas.
A rhumba of rattlesnakes.
A bed of eels.
A quiver of cobras.
A generation of vipers.
A cloud of grasshoppers.
A plague of locusts.
An army of caterpillars.
A consortium of octopuses.
An audience of squids.
An escargatoire of snails.
A risk of lobsters.
A blush of boys.
A faith of merchants.
A superfluity of nuns
A cabal of Karens.
Oh yes.
I'm counting you humans in this game.
You find ways to group each other in words,
In ways elegant, and in ways crass.
Like.

Chink.
That one I've heard plenty of times behind the ears
Of the Chinese baby boy.

A burp is heard.

But for me.
Cockroach.
Guess what word is used to group us?
Guess.

An intrusion of cockroaches.

Wooop, sorry, outta the way,
Imma be here INTRUDING.
You wanted to get that bag of ketchup chips,
WOOOP, sorry,
Got here first,
Finders keepers.
Awww,
You thought the bathroom was the only place to take a shit?

Sorry, babe,
I had to go on your rotisserie chicken.

An intrusion.

And so,
When you call other humans cockroaches,
You imply they're intruding,
You imply they need to get the fuck out
And set up walls between them and us.
You need to find ways to STOP THEM FROM COMING IN.

And here in Hong Kong,
Having spent years in this home,
With this Chinese baby,
I sense what intrusion means.

I see how this city, this city of outcasts,
Is fought over,
How the Brits and the Chinese go at it,
How their own citizens,
How the locals,
How a whole population of Hong Kong born and raised,
Are becoming outsiders.
Intruders.
In their own city, by the people who run it.

You strip intruders of their humanity by stripping them of their rights.
And that's what's happening to the humans in Hong Kong.
Being reduced to cockroaches.

So where's a roach like me gonna go?

COCKROACH lights up another catnip joint.

I'm leaving.
And truss me.
I'll miss the heat.
I'll miss the humidity.
I'll miss the neon lights and the buffet of street stalls.
I'll miss being able to visit my mother's ooo sac grave.
And send blessings to my twelve siblings.

But I gotta survive.
I gotta taste the world.
I gotta live the dream that I envisioned for Rosie and me.

And like Mama Blatta's trip from
Whitney's wig from Houston to Hong Kong,
Imma have the adventure of a lifetime,
Tucked away in baby boy's underwear.

Packed myself plenty of catnip for the trip.
But ya know, I'm living it up,
I'm moving, I'm hustling,
I'm gonna keep living.
I'm gonna inherit the earth.
And—

BOY
Be to be to be to be to be to be to be to be to be to be to—

A burp is heard.

chapter 2—the Bard

Suddenly COCKROACH speaks in a thick Cantonese accent.

COCKROACH
And I'm gonna DREAM the life
And LIVE the dream and
And . . .

Beat.

What happening?

Beat.

Do you . . .
Is it just me?
Why I sound like?

Beat.

What the actual fuck?
Why I sound Chinese?!

The BARD enters,
Who's basically COCKROACH,
Who's basically the BOY.
Just that, the BARD finally emerges.

BARD

Lo, in the orient when the gracious light
Lifts up his burning head, each under eye
Doth homage to his new-appearing sight—

COCKROACH

Oh. My. God.
Get. The. Fuck. OUT.
I tell you,
Every time I about to FLY into my DREAMS,
This cracker-ass bitch,
He just come on in
And he say so many so so many word with
No meaning.

BARD

Told by an idiot, full of sound and fury,
Signifying nothing.
You sure you're not talking 'bout yourself, boy?

COCKROACH

EVERY TIME.
I tell my story,
This dude, he jump in,
He come in and interrupt
And he poem poem poem
And is like,
Dude, I just cockroach,
You go eat your fish and chip
And leave me alone!

BARD

They've heard enough from you, boy.

COCKROACH
NEVER.
And stop calling me BOY.
I COCKROACH, NO BOY.

Beat.

I have I have
So much left to share,
So much story.

Beat.

I have not tell them about when I FLY to Canada
And meet Rosie 2.0 and Rosie 3.0
And magical place in Canada call Red Lobster!
And the Canada
So many snow
So much new new new
So not like Hong Kong
So comfortable.

BARD
Hush, BOY.
No matter where; of comfort no man speak:
Let's talk of graves, of worms, and epitaphs;
Make dust our paper and with rainy eyes
Write sorrow on the bosom of the earth.

BARD takes a bow.

It's my turn, bitches.
To be
To be
To be
Me.

Take a guess,
An educated guess.
Can you imagine,
If I came back to life
And spoke with all of you gathered
Like JAYYYYSUS risen,
Or Beyoncé at Coachella,
Or, I dunno,
Just imagine anyone you worship,
Alive or otherwise,
In front of you,
Telling you a story.

COCKROACH
BILL.
YOU SIMPLY BILL.
STUPID BILL.
JUST AS BAD AS BILL BELL—

BARD
I said hush.
To be me,
William Shakespeare—

COCKROACH
(keeps speaking until interrupted) BILL BILL BILL BILL BILL—

BARD
Billy for short.

Beat.

To. Be. Me.

Beat.

It's quite a conundrum, you see.
Think of my name,
Then think of a saying.
Any saying.
More than likely I invented the fucker.

Beat.

Let's . . . Break the ice, shall we?
See?
I wrote that in *Shrew*.

Beat.

And now you sit there,
Anticipating the next thing,
My next thought, my next word with
. . . bated breath.

Beat.

Merchant of Venice.

Beat.

But of course,
Though you may worship me,
And let's be honest,
You do, you have such money flowing in my name
That you'd think I'm the be-all and end-all of the written word

Beat.

Merchant, again.

Beat.

Though, come what may.

Beat.

Mac . . .

COCKROACH
Mac . . . ?
Mackers
MacBook Pro
MAC Cosmetics
*Mac*Donald's
MAC (Musée d'art contemporain)
What the fuck are you saying—

BARD
*Mac*FUCKING*beth.*
GASP.
I SAID IT.
I SAID THE M word.
FOR GOODNESS' SAKE, I CAN'T BELIEVE BILLY SAID—

Beat.

For goodness' sake.
Henry VIII.

Beat.

But truth be told,
In my heart of hearts—

BOY
Hamlet . . .

Beat.

BARD
I find myself in a bit of a pickle.

Beat.

The Tempest.

Beat.

Beyond any rhyme or reason.

Beat.

Twelfth Night.

Beat.

You circulate my words,
My thoughts,
My plays,
My stories,
My being,
My very self,
My views,
Like a plague.
I mean, think.
Just think.
How many of your thoughts are truly your own
If so many of the words you use to think,
Draws from me?
Can there be too much of a good thing?

Beat.

As You Like It.

Beat.

Between each of you,
Between the words you share amongst yourselves,
In your shortened tweeted ways of speaking,
Your little LOL lingo,
Your BRBs and WTFs,
Your LMFAOs.
Between the ways you find connection
And express your tears
Or your laughs
Or your aches,
If all of these . . .
Letters and words
Stem from me,
Then . . .
My gosh, is there a bit of me in you?
Every one of you?
If so, the world's truly my oyster, isn't it?

Beat.

Merry Wives of Windsor.

Beat.

It's as if in my mind's eye—

BOY
Hamlet . . .

Beat.

BARD
I see this as naked truth.

Beat.

Love's Labour's Lost.

Beat.

The truth that you're all a little bit
My own flesh and blood—

COCKROACH
Hamlet.

Beat.

BARD
You may not carry my genetics,
Or my dashing good looks,
Or my frilly fashion sense with my sexy-ass pantaloons
And fucked-up teeth.
But you carry my words,
Which means I live in your brain rent free,
In your mind,
In your dreams,
In your very way of being.
And parents do love their children—

COCKROACH
MAMA BLATTA LOVE ME.
SHE LOVE ME,
SHE JUST COULD NOT SURVIVE THE POWER WASH.

BARD
Oh shut up, boy,
You're the laughingstock of us all.

Beat.

Haha.
Laughingstock.
Merry Wives of Windsor.
See what I mean?!

Beat.

As MOST parents, barring Mama Blatta,
Love their children,
So do I love you.
And truly,
Love is blind.

Beat.

Merchant.

Beat.

And with my blind love,
I must wear my heart on my sleeve.

Beat.

Othello.

Beat.

I love you.
For still reading my shit.
I mean, most writers,
They write these things and they die as they live,
And my gosh,
To think you all would keep my stupid-ass stories around.
Like I mean, seriously,
Have you read *Midsummer Night's Dream*?
I wrote a posse of fairies with stupid-ass names
And all of you put this play on and like the fairies are
ELOCUTING
And ARTICULATING
And prim and proper.
THEY'RE FAIRIES.

And ya know, things shift,
And there's a line in that play,
I meant no offence, truly, none at all,
The Orientals have some really great food like
Dumplings and like noodles, and like wonton soup,
But this line,
"The Chink in the wall."

A grunt is heard.

Gosh,
You gotta stop saying that.

COCKROACH
IT'S RACIAL.
I am born Hong Kong,
I am CHINESE.

BARD
Exactly what that thing said.
Words change, you know this.
And my gosh, I did not intend for that word to become
What do you say,
A slur?
So please. Play nice.
Just change it.
I personally like the kink ON the wall,
Cuz ask any of your gay friends about holes in walls,
Which is . . . basically what my line is about,
And
You'll get some particularly fascinating and . . . potentially educational stories.

Beat.

Anyway,
It's a true honour.
I love you *all* for that.

Beat.

But I must confess.
I'm dead.
Like dust-to-dust dead.
Yet every fucking time you mutter something I wrote,
My spirit gets conjured back
And I have to sit there
Watching THESPIANS or high schoolers alike
Tackle THE SPEECH.

Beat.

Please.
Get rid of me.
GOOD RIDDANCE, you should say,
And I know some of you do,
So thank you.

Beat.

Oh yes, good riddance,
Merchant.

Beat.

And as much as some of you say
"KILL HIS PLAYS.
NO MORE SHAKESPEARE SEASONS.
DON'T TEACH HIS SHIT NO MORE."
Which I am totally in agreement with, truly,
It doesn't matter.
It doesn't.

Unless you were to completely change the language,
Change this English,
Change the idioms,
The phrases,
The casual sayings entirely,
My spidey senses tingle each and every time
You start a joke with
KNOCK KNOCK!

COCKROACH
WHAT THE FUCK YOU WANT?

BARD
. . . Who's there?—

COCKROACH
What?—

BARD
After I say "knock knock,"
You gotta say "who's there"—

COCKROACH & BOY
NO!

BARD and COCKROACH both catch the BOY's intrusion.

Beat.

BARD
Anyway,
Wrote that one in *Mackers*.

Beat.

I implore you,
Kill me with kindness.

Beat.

Shrew.

Beat.

To thine own self be true—

BOY
Hamlet—

COCKROACH
How original—

BARD
(to COCKROACH) I'm just so quotable, ya know?

Beat.

(to audience) Think for yourself.
I'll still creep in one way or another, I know.
Gosh that's exciting, really, it is.
I know I wrote about anything, and everything,
But the memes, the gifs, the things I can't even put into words,
Or other languages,
My gosh,
They let me sleep.
Perchance to dream,
Or perchance to simply sleep.

COCKROACH
Nuh uh,
No you did not, Billy.
You did not write everything.

BARD
'Scuse me?
I did.
How dare you?
The academia states that I am simply, factually
UNIVERSAAAAL.

COCKROACH
No.

BARD
Well like, yea, like I probably didn't write about
Bitcoin or like flying cars and shit I couldn't have imagined,
But like all the human emotions, all that inner-world stuff,
I'm pretty damn sure I was pretty thorough.

COCKROACH
You missed me.

BARD
What the fuck you going on about?

COCKROACH
You never wrote about me.

BARD
Bees,
Maggots,
And the poor beetle that we tread upon
In corporal sufferance finds a pang as great
As when a giant dies.

Beat.

For so work the honeybees,
Creatures that by a rule in nature
Teach the act of order to a peopled kingdom.

Beat.

If I be waspish, best beware my sting.

COCKROACH
On and on, bugs and maggots of all nature, but
But you never once, ever, used the word cockroach.
How ironic, given that your words
Live like a cockroach,
You never once mention me.
Why?

BARD
I.
Hm.
I never thought of you.
Hence, I never wrote you.

COCKROACH
There are a lot of things you did not think about,
Hence you never wrote about.

BARD
I'M UNIVERSAL.

COCKROACH
But, like, no.
You tell stories of what you know,
Or imagined, within the realm of what you know,
And everything and anything beyond that,
Like about chinks—

A grunt is heard.

Or cockroaches,
Or boys stuck in sticky situations,
That's . . .
Your stories do not speak for us all.

BARD
My work was words.
You have taken them far away to do things
I never intended.

COCKROACH
Oh yes.
Like to tell who is smarter than who.
Like to say who's human and who's not.
Like to conquer and wield as a greater species.

The weight of your stories
Swallows the expanse of
This dream.

BARD
Unintentional
Collateral
Damage.

COCKROACH
And your Lear,
Or your Big Mac
Or your Hamlet.

It dwarfs Mama Blatta and her journey across the seas.
The story of a cockroach,
The story of Rosie,
The story of a boy.

BARD
Tell your own stories,
I long for it.
Share it, breathe it out, and kill Lear.
The old man deserves a rest.

COCKROACH
Yet some old man,
Somewhere in the world,
Will still watch *Lear* and weep.

BARD
If that's what comes from hearing the story,
Then so be it.

COCKROACH
And the story I've shared,
The life of a cockroach,
What do you make of that?

BARD
It's not my business to make anything of it.
You tell the story,
And it does what it needs to for you, and you alone.

COCKROACH
Then why tell any stories?

BARD
Then why live?
Then why laugh?
Then why cry?
Then why?
Why?

COCKROACH
To begin and to end?

BARD
To escape
To distract
To dream
To become something other than
To imagine something other than
To understand something other than /
To rest
To hope
To enact
To respond
To demolish
To delight
To to to . . .
To be to be to be.

The BOY *whispers in unison, beginning after the forward slash and continuing until the end of the* BARD*'s line.*

BOY
To be to be to be to be to be to be . . .

Beat.

COCKROACH
A story of a cockroach
Encountering the story of a bard
Is a story about a boy.

BARD
About a boy who has yet to understand
That this moment
Will ripple across time
And hold him in place
Paralyzed
Till he can tell it
Till he can speak it out

Release it
Share it
And move on.
To understand that this
This moment
Speaks to his very being.
To be.
To be him.

Beat.

Building suspense, now, aren't we, li'l roach?
Just WHAT
GASP
Are we talking about?!

Beat.

We're skirting around it, aren't we?

COCKROACH
Don't go there. Not yet.

BARD
Is he all right?

COCKROACH
I don't know.

BARD
You're him.

COCKROACH
As are you.

BARD
Alas, the day.

COCKROACH
Don't start.

BARD
We must. Sooner or later.
We must let him tell his story.

COCKROACH
Through you, ironically.

BARD
Through you, understandably.

COCKROACH
It's why they're all there.

BARD
It's already started.
This is all part of it.
Your story,
My story,
His story.
All one.

COCKROACH
The stories we tell ourselves
When we'd rather not live the one we're living.

BARD
We are stories.
To be a story is to be to be . . .

chapter 3—the Boy

The feeling of a car crash,
Of some inescapable doom,
Some self-perpetuated prison walls
Crumbling.

Really, though,
It's a boy
In the throes of an attempt.

It's the boy going through
A trauma
That ignites
Self-dehumanization
In order to survive
This present moment.

That feeling,
When something so horrific has happened,
A passing,
A disaster,
An assault.

And the only way to breathe through it
Is to pretend,
Imagine,
Figure any which way
To not be there,
To separate

Mind,
Soul,
From body.

The splinters get stuck.
Trauma sweeps in at moments.
So confusing is the ordeal.

We hear the story
Of how the BOY *got here.*
Backwards.
It is intoned, almost chanted, at a rapid pace.

BOY
Be to not or be to
Was whisper could I
All nightmare the during
Here? Get I did how
Something.
Anything.
For scramble I.
This than sweeter
Is thought other any
Smiling stop I
Out walk I
Okay not am I

A disgusting sound.

COCKROACH
TSO LA
TSO LA
TSO LA
LAI HEUNG DOW MMUN MUT YEA
AH?!
[Run
Run

Run
What are you doing?!]

BOY
Okay not am I
Smile I
Burps he
Rush head
Poppers choose I

A disgusting sound.

COCKROACH
DIU.
Lai heung dow jow mut yea tze?!
[Fuck.
What are you doing?!]

BOY
Smile.

Beat.

(in the man's voice) "Does my boy want some?"

Powder white
Poppers
Needles
These out takes
Him owe I guess
Me fed he but

Okay not was I.

COCKROACH
Tso la tso la tso la
Lai jeung yow see gan ah.
[Run run run
You still have time to run.]

BOY
Okay.

Eight?
Mhmm.
Ten?
Younger.
Fourteen?
Younger.
Sixteen?

Sure. Smile.

"Wanna be younger for me?"

COCKROACH
GET THE FUCK OUT.

BOY
Me to doesn't matter
Say you thank
Younger look you
Come off shirts
And pants the
Done lobster
Like smells Scotia Nova what that is
Night the throughout me over

All burps
Gassy him makes
Full me makes
Delicious
Butter
Garlic with lobster
Yes. Yes.
"You hungry?"

COCKROACH
Diu
Lai tse dow tow aw ga
[Why are you always so hungry?]

BOY
Lobster Scotian Nova
Something like it's

Lobster some
Out takes he

Wait I
Wait
Hunger . . .
Of sort that not

"You gotta eat me up, boy."

Okay.

COCKROACH
GO.
RUN.
GO.
RUN.

BOY
Being trumps hunger
Hungry was but
Wait
Buzzer
Three storeys
La Fontaine Parc by
Apartment the find

Bixi or
STM
To broke too

Over walk
Off name
Off earring
Off glasses
Down dress
Or
Up dress
Time it's

COCKROACH
Mmm how tzai tee gan
[Don't waste time.]

BOY
Work home
Do gotta
Friends tell
I hang to time no
Over school's
Me of sale
Successful sale
Made bid

Go I work to
Work to work to
To to to

A disgusting sound.

(During the nightmare
All I could whisper was)

To be or not to be
To be or not to be
To be or not to be
That is the—

COCKROACH
Diu, lei jou me jung heung do ah?
Tso la,
Tso la,
Tso la.
Yow ma yea mmmn tai tze?
[Fuck, why are you still here?
Run,
Run,
Run.
What question?]

What question you dumb fuck
What question what question
No question
Run run run get out
Of here
Move run run run
Out of your skin
Out of your yellow
Run run run run

Why the fuck are you reciting Shakespeare
When you're in the middle of being—

Sharp inhale.
Continues:

BOY
Whether 'tis nobler in the mind—

COCKROACH
Noble
Noble
Far from
Noble
Your pants down
Your eyes shut
Your mouth covered
Your nose tightened
To cut out that . . . awful smell.

You idiot
What nobility can you afford
When it's not just that dumb-ass bard melting your language
When you lost your ability to dream in your mother tongue
Do you remember when that was?
Do you remember when you forgot?
Do you remember how?
Do you remember that instance when dreams
When dreams
Shifted from Chinese
To English
When even your dreams became colonized and you forgot your tongue?

Beat.

Just like in
GRADE FIVE
Remember?
Your first year in this
OOOOOOOH CANADA
OUR HOME AND—

When you mistook blackmail
For Black males
For that confidence you showed
Your hand raised
Your little glimmer of pride
Squeaking up and saying,
"Oh I got this.
I know a little bit of this English.
I know a little bit of what it means to speak like the rest of you all."

But little
That's the key word
Little
You know so little
You know so little
And you'll always know so little
Cuz this world is not for you.

BOY
Whether 'tis nobler in the mind to suffer
The slings and arrows of outrageous fortune—

COCKROACH
Oh what fortune
What fortune
When you bought that bag from Hong Kong
Brought it back
And everyone on the TTC thought
Damn crazy rich Asian

When you thought yourself
Damn
I'm not like those other Chinese
Look at my bag
I'm adjusted
I'm assimilated
Look at me
I'm one of you all because my bag
The dollar dollar bling bling on it
Some badge
Some armour
That you'd thought would protect you?
Protect you from the the the truth that
Protection is afforded the rich
It's afforded the white
It's afforded when you can pay
And the currency isn't money
It's not how much you spend
Or how much you make
It's how much you hate
This world of hate
This world that grew you from love
Only to age
And become an adult
And find
How hate governs as the prime currency of being
And now you stand
Thinking some bag
Will show the world
The dollar dollar bling bling of your existence.

But you'll never be enough.
You know this.
You dream this.
You walk with this.

And when the bag falls,
When by the doors of the TTC,
When it's screamed at you:

(a Karen voice, North American accent) Um . . .
'Scuse me.
You know it's like
Illegal for you to stand
By the door.
You're IN THE WAY.
I don't know where you come from,
Young man,
But like,
It's illegal.
So
Move,
Just move,
Move away from the door,
Or I'll call the cops,
And I'll like—

Beat.

Do you like
Even speak English?
Lemme say it again:
YOU'RE IN THE WAY.
MOVE.
And while you're at it:
GO HOME.

(COCKROACH voice, Cantonese accent) Go home go home go home go home
. . . And we did nothing

BARD
You did nothing.

Beat.

COCKROACH
All your preparation
All your wit
And smarts
And education and
Wokeness
And all your awoken
Fight and flight
As some pasty-ass crusty woman stares down the barrel of your eye slits and says to you
"Go home"
You just stood
Mouth agape
Cavernous mouth of silence
No answer.

BARD
Why didn't I answer?

COCKROACH
Why didn't you tell her to fuck off or fuck herself?
Why didn't you tell anyone?

BARD
Why didn't you ask me for help?

COCKROACH
Because
Because

You know
You are nothing more than a cockroach
And she's right
It's not your home
It's not your home
You're a cockroach
You're an intrusion.

BOY
Or to take arms against a sea of trouble—

BARD
Double, double toil and TROUBLE
Mmmmmmmm.
The
De dum de dum de dum de dum de dum
Of the drum
Of my words
The metre
The iambic
The pentameter
The verse
The good
The perfect
The way to write
The way to speak
The way to speak the DNA of this tongue
The molecules shift rage running whirlwind tsunami waterfall crash of sound
Raging up and up and up from
Your throat up and up through your—

BOY
And by opposing, end them.

BARD
If you're gonna speak my verse,
DO IT RIGHT.

Beat.

Stand straight stand still
Stand there
Stand here
Stand wherever
I say
You stand
You dumb fuck butt-fuck
Chink

I am
I have
Done this for so long
I know
I know
How
You must
Speak
My tongue
My words
As such
It is law
It is mandate
It is what it is
To question me
Is futile
Like questioning why the sun shines
Like why the clouds cry
Like why the world could care less of your yellow your yellow your yellow

The skin of you
So so despicable
So like jaundice
So like foo man chu
So like the ones who take them jobs
So like that model minority
SO BE SUBMISSIVE
BE A GOOD LITTLE BOY
Take me in
Fill it up so you can let the white
From inside
Slowly erode the yellow
Outside
No question
No questions
Just be. A. Good. Chinky. Boy.

BOY
To die, to sleep . . .

Beat.

NO MORE.
Get out get out get out
Of my FUCKING HEAD.
LEAVE ME ALONE.

Advising like the worst acting teacher
You've ever met:

BARD
STAY ON THE TEXT,
BOY.
How dare you disrespect the TEXT.
The metre is so delicate,
Allllll the damned clues
Can be found in my words.

It's between the cracks,
Through the elisions,
The thesis,
And the antithesis,
The

Beat.

Caesuras,
The elongated vowels of OOOOO,
The IMAGES,
The verse,
The rhythm,
The FOLIOS,
The Stratford strut,
The putting on of that
CLASSICAL VOICE,
The

Take a look at the last words of each verse line.
It contains worlds of its own.

Take a look at this

Beat.

Caesura.

It contains laws of its own.

Look at the beauty of these eleven beats.
It means I'm rushing with such thought
I can barely contain my PASSIONS
In TEN.

Take a look at your body.
God! Boy,

Stop moving so much,
SHAKESPEARE SHOULD BE DELIVERED
LIKE TALKING FUCKING HEADS.
LET THE WORDS LIVE.
LET IT RING THROUGH THE HALLS,
CONJURING TEARS AND EMOOOOOTIONS
AND ALL THE PRESTIGE OF MY GENIUS.

I am the metre stick,
The test,
The be all.
If y'all got nuked today,
I'd still outlive
Every single
One of you.

COCKROACH
I'd outlive you,
Cracker-ass bisexual ghost.
I'd outlive you
And your rhymes,
Your HILLLLARIOUS jokes,
So funny I can already hear the snoring
Before you even dipped your white wood
In black ink—
Scribbled shit across pages and called it
ART,
THEATRE,
PSYCHOLOGY OF THE WESTERN WORLD,
GREATEST LIVING WRITER OF THE HUMAN RACE,
Before any of your laws
And decrees
And rules.

I was already here.

甲由.
[Cockroach.]

None of y'all can see how my name is written.
It no fit in your alphabet.
It'd get lost within your WEAK twenty-six letters
Our words are lines.
They are symbols.
They grow beyond letters
Because the world so vast,
So mysterious,
So gigantic,
So inexplicable,
How can you contain all the magic
In twenty-six symbols?

WE HAVE TWO HUNDRED WAYS OF WRITING
ONE WORD.
AND WE DO NOT NEED SO MANY WORDS TO SAY
ONE THING.
ALL YOUR TO BE OR NOT TO BE,
ALL YOUR REFLECTION IN THE DARK
AGAINST THE MOON,
WE'VE ALREADY DONE IT
A THOUSAND YEAR BEFORE YOU,
CRACKER ASS:

床前明月光，
疑是地上霜。
举头望明月，
低头思故乡。

chuáng qián míng yuè guāng
yí shì dì shang shuāng
jǔ tóu wàng míng yuè
dī tóu sī gù xiāng

I'm basically like, a million years old,
So tuck your baby-ass five-hundred-year-old English self
Into bed,
Shakespeare.
You ain't no authority on long lives.

BOY
SHUT UP.

Beat.

. . . And by a sleep to say we end
The heartache, and the thousand natural shocks
That flesh is heir to. 'Tis a consummation
Devoutly to be wish'd. To die, to sleep—
To sleep—perchance to dream. Ay, there's the rub . . .

BARD
Back in my day,
We certainly didn't rub it out
Quite like that.

We hear a disgusting sound.
A pause as the BARD takes this in.

BOY
No more.
Please.
No more.

BARD
What is that he's doing now?

That's quite the technique he's got there.
Impressive stroke game,
Wouldn't you say?

COCKROACH
I wouldn't know.
Humans copulate
In the weirdest ways.

Beat.

BARD
I can't tell,
My boy.
Is this pain or pleasure?

BOY
STOP.
STOP.
STOP.
LET ME GO.
STOP.

BARD
Pain.
Certainly, pain.

COCKROACH
Pain.
Such pain.

BOY
It hurts.
Please,
I didn't ask for this,
This wasn't—

COCKROACH
This was exactly what you asked for.
You got yourself into this.
You walked through those doors,

You looked him in the eyes,
And you agreed to this—

BOY
I did—did—did
Not
Agree to to to to to
I I I

COCKROACH
Always I
Always you
Always that first word
Always that first
Identification
That identity starts with I
How true
How flawlessly honest
How coincidental
How I defines you
How I is nothing more
Than a single letter that explodes
Into orientation
The orient of your face
The sexuality of your body
The submission of your race
The I
Defines each and every one of you
And me
So let's not lie
To each other
I
Am more
Than you
Yet your I
Will always feel more than someone else's.

And that is not wrong.
It *is*.
Admit it.

BOY
For who would bear the whips and scorns of time,
The oppressor's wrong, the proud man's contumely,
The pangs of despised love, the law's delay,
The insolence of office, and the spurns
That patient merit of the unworthy takes,
When he himself might his quietus make.

COCKROACH
What the FUCK IS A QUIETUS?
When this chink learned it,
He thought it meant to shut the f up.
What does that word even mean?!

BARD
I dunno.
Sounded cool when I wrote it.

COCKROACH
It's confusing.

BARD
I needed a word to fit the metre.
To fit the rhyme.

COCKROACH
And I need you to listen to yourself
And hear how ridiculous you sound.

BARD
It means
He is quit.

COCKROACH
How fitting.
Our boy is certainly quitting himself.

BARD
No,
He's not.
He has my words to hold him.

COCKROACH
No,
Your words are part of
How he got himself into this.

BARD
Not my fault
He reveres me.

COCKROACH
He has no choice.
The world tells him to revere you.

BARD
Not once in my life, or in my present
Ghostly
State,
Did I expect
A boy to conjure me while he's . . .

BOY
But that the dread of something after death,
The undiscover'd country, from whose bourn

COCKROACH
Yes . . . yes . . .
This undiscover'd country you've found yourself in,
This land of red-and-white leaves,

These Westerners that hug as if human contact
Was a scarcity.
This land that taught you how to smile to appear less threatening,
This land that asked you to change your name
For fear of confusion,
This land that has given you the opportunity
To realize your dreams . . .
Discover your loves and fears
In this undiscover'd country.

BOY
And thus the native hue of resolution

A grunt.

Is sicklied o'er with the pale cast of thought

COCKROACH
Pale cast of thought? Native hue?! Damn, you racist!
Yow mow gow tscho?
[Are you fucking kidding me?]
HOW ABOUT IF WE HAVE A YELLOW CAST OF THOUGHT?

BARD
Like I said,
Never meant my words for you.
Thoughts are much more compelling
When spoken by pale pasty meatheads like me.

BOY
And enterprises of great pith and moment,
With this regard, their currents turn awry,
And lose the name of—

BARD
Action. Now's the time for action.

COCKROACH
BOY. WATCH OUT.
HE'S GOING TO CHOKE YOU.

The disgusting sound
Re-emerges, full throttle.

BARD
Twist your head the other way, boy!

COCKROACH
Face the wall, boy!

BARD
Don't let him see the fear, boy!

COCKROACH
Bite the pillow, boy!

BARD
Fight him, boy!

COCKROACH
Fight him!

BARD
Fight!

COCKROACH
FIGHT.

BOY
Thus conscience does make cowards of us all

COCKROACH
STOP BEING A COWARD.
WHEN HE COMES,
KICK HIM IN THE BALLS.

BARD
RUN, BOY.
RUN.

COCKROACH
Pick yourself up and fight.

BARD
Release yourself from this this nightmare.

COCKROACH
Free yourself.

BARD
Fend for yourself.

COCKROACH
He's moaning.
Do it.
Cut him up.
Make him feel what he's made you feel.

BARD
Act.
Do something.

COCKROACH
Your actions led you here,
Now your actions will dictate
How you leave.

BARD
He's moaning.
Do it.
Cut him up.
Make him suffer.

COCKROACH
Grab the needle,
Slide it into his eyes.

BARD
Blind him with the white powder he ingests.

COCKROACH
Pop those poppers up his popper.
Take the lobster,
Chuck it at his face.

BARD
Cuff him to his bed,
Leave him here chained
So that when his wife finds him
He'll have to explain himself outta the closet.

COCKROACH
Put on your pants.

BARD
Put on your shirt.

COCKROACH
RUN FOR THE DOOR.

BARD
Walk, don't run,
Don't let him smell your fear.

COCKROACH
Why are you shaking his hand, BOY?

BARD
Polite
Even in the face of perverts.

COCKROACH
WHY ARE YOU SMILING, BOY?

BARD
The etiquette of the orient.
You would know, Cockroach.
Such a submissive race.

COCKROACH
That's an excuse.
Not a submissive race,
Just a submissive boy:

Like with Grandma . . .

When your own
Back home
Neglect you.

When Grandma
Miraculously misses putting up a picture of you
Amongst her twenty-five grandchildren.
And when you ask why
All she says is:

"There's no space for all my grandchildren."

BARD
And in that answer lies the truth
There is no space for all her grandchildren
And this world has no space for all the children
And who chooses whose children belongs in which space
Which land
Which country
When people pillage each other
When countries torn
Tearing at the borders
When walls have become hope for some
When saying no to compassion
They take it all
When this is the world as it stands.

COCKROACH
It feels very much that Grandma not having space
For a small picture of you on her cupboard says it all
Says it all
And the truth that you know
That it's because, what you're a fag?
In her eyes, a shame, a blemish.

BARD
A shadow shaded
Oh . . . boy
Your sea of troubles is but a droplet
Not even
A molecule
In the ocean of hopelessness
The inevitable thaw of the north
The point of no return for us all
Will pass and so
Taking arms against a sea of trouble seems
Futile, doesn't it?

Cockroach.
Let's cross our arms.
Sit back
Chill
Relax
It'll all end anyway.
He's gonna do
Nothing.

The boy lashes out.
The sound hides for a moment.
He whimpers.
He gets stuffed against the wall.

It is so painful
That no sound exists
That can articulate that hurt.

So we face silence.
(For as long as the silence can be
Sustained.)

COCKROACH and BARD
Reach out:

COCKROACH
I was born when you were born.
A little cockroach
On a lifetime Disney ride with a little
Chinky baby.

I was there that moment of birth.
I was there for the first cry,
Roar, inhale of breath.
I was there that first night you slept,
That you felt a dream.

I was there,
And I sang to you:

(in a lullaby-like tone to a baby boy) Oh, little baby
Oh, little baby
What will come
The dreams
The hopes
The wishes
The joys
The love
The fear
The all
The beginning
The ending
The foods
The laughs
The cries
The wail
The breath
The thing—

BARD
That that that
Will grow
To / be

COCKROACH
Be stunted
The being
The wanting
The craving
The hunger
The sound
The family
The friends
The exes and enemies

The thing the thing
The everything
The nothing
The music
Oh the music

Beat.

Oh the music

Beat.

The lies
The truth
The flying
The skin
The coming into yellow—

BARD
The dissolving into white—

COCKROACH
The brain
The brawn
The hair
The hair
How you'll have a little time of brown
Only to return to black

BARD
Mostly out of laziness—

COCKROACH
But a return to black
The rhythms
The key
The dancing of feet

Of smiles
Of tears that drop
Pitter patter pitter patter
Up against your eyes
The dark
The light
The things

I promise
I promise
Little baby
I promise
Beyond me,
Beyond breath,
Beyond the nest,
The all,
I will
Always always always—

BARD
That's a lie—

COCKROACH
Not always.
You will certainly be alone at times,
But always
I'll follow you,
And I will catch you in your dreams,
And I will hush your nightmares calm.
I will always sit in a corner of your dark,
Bright mind,
Behind your eyes,
At the tip of your tongue,
The front and back and veil of the brow.
I will always be with you.
That much, I promise.
Hush.

BARD
Hush.

COCKROACH
Hush.

Pause.

BARD
I had two major lovers in my life.

COCKROACH
The raven-haired beauty, and . . . ?

BARD
Some boy.

Beat.

Wrote a bunch of rhymes to the both of them,
Charting out my ecstatic, obsessive, terrifying
Experiences of love and lust.

Every sting,
Every rejection,
Every wall that I faced in consummating these loves,
Was an ill I would bear.

And for each accumulating illness of love,
I would try to find my way back,
Find my way home,
To the heart,
To the light.

COCKROACH
But it is hard
When you've travelled into such . . .

BARD
Pain . . .
That it'll be impossible
For you to travel back into innocence alone.

I am here,
My boy.

Let me bear this ill for you
However I can.

COCKROACH
He doesn't need you to bear anything,
Bard.
He will survive this.
All this
Has brought you here.
All this
You must endure.
And after this
You walk out,
You clean yourself off,
You keep breathing.
You must, my boy.
My life depends on yours.

BARD
Oh boy oh boy oh boy,
This is but one calamity of your young young life.

Beat.

At my deathbed,
I thought to myself,
"Great,
I've written some plays,
I've given Queen Lizzie some royal headaches,

I've INVENTED so so so many words
For all y'all lazy-ass anglophones.
Great,
Let's pass on quietly,
And live in that post-dream death forever and ever . . . "

I will live as long as my words exist,
And that
Is a calamity for a ghost like me.

As for you,
My seventeen-year-old boy.
You will outlive your calamity.
I promise you.

Leave my words to rest.
Find your own.

The boy finds his words.
Tells his story.

BOY
To work
To work
To work I go

Bid made
Sale successful
Sale of me.
School's over.
No time to hang,
I tell friends.
Gotta do homework.

It's time.
Dress up.
Or

Dress down.
Glasses off
Earring off
Name off.
Walk over.

Too broke to STM.
Or Bixi.

Find the apartment.
By Parc La Fontaine.
Three storeys.
Buzzer.
Wait.

Beat.

Buzzer broken, he says.

Comes to get me.
White tank top,
Shorts.
Forget the colour,
Too dark anyway.

I smile.
All starts with the smile.
Lie about my age.

Yes. Legal.
I say.

Doesn't matter to me, he says.

Okay.

I was not okay.
Was hungry.
Hunger trumps being okay.

"You gotta eat me up, boy."

Not that sort of hunger . . .

"Wait."

I wait.

He takes out some lobster.

It's like
Nova Scotian lobster.

"On sale at marché."
"You hungry?"

Yes.
Yes.
Lobster with garlic butter.
Delicious.
Makes me full.
Makes him gassy.

Burps all over me throughout the night.

Is that what Nova Scotia smells like?

I've never been.

Lobster done,
The pants and shirts come off.

"You look younger than you say."

No shit, Sherlock.

No, I'm eighteen, I say.

"Doesn't matter to me."
"Wanna be younger for me?"

Sixteen?

"Younger."

Fourteen?

"Younger."

Ten?

"Younger."

Eight?

Pause.

"Okay."

I was not okay.

But he fed me.
Guess I owe him.

Takes out these needles,
Poppers,
White powder?

"Does my boy want some?

Pause.

No.
No.
Smile.
No.
Not part of the deal.

He takes them.
I had to take one.
I choose poppers.
Head rush.

He burps.
I smile.
I am not okay.

He thrusts.
I smile.
He smacks.
I smile.
He calls me like a pet.
I smile.
I am not okay.
He pays up.

Thank you.
Food for a while.

"Now get out of my house."

Door slams.

The scene shifts
To outside the apartment.

COCKROACH
Walk out of here.

BOY
I walk out of the apartment.
I stop smiling.

BARD
Covert enmity under the smile of safety
Wounds the world.

BOY
Any other thought is sweeter than this.

BARD
Sweets to the sweet, my boy.

BOY
I scramble for anything.
Something.

COCKROACH
You want poutine
From La Banquise
On your walk home?

BARD
HOW ARE YOU STILL HUNGRY, BOY?!

COCKROACH
It is hard work,
Selling yourself.

BOY
No,
I'm not hungry.
I'm just . . .

How . . .
How can I end this?

COCKROACH
There is no ending this.
That is not your job.
You just keep walking
Forward,
You keep breathing.
That's all.
There is no ending this.

BOY
This man . . .
This . . .
This was never part of the dream—

COCKROACH
Do not let this become a nightmare—

BOY
During the nightmare, all I could whisper was:

BARD
My words.
All you could whisper were my words.
Now you have your own.

BOY
How do I survive this?

COCKROACH
You already have.

BOY
I don't understand / how—

BARD
Give it an understanding, but no tongue.

Beat.

BOY
I—

COCKROACH
Shut the fuck up.
I hate you more.

BOY
I'm alive.

BARD
You are the cruellest *he* alive.
Changed it just for you, my boy.

BOY
I want home.

COCKROACH
Go home.
Go home.
Go home.
Go home.
Go home.

BOY
. . . How?

COCKROACH
Chuang Qian Ming—

BARD
Let me.

COCKROACH
What the fuck?

BARD
Time for this old dog to learn some new poems,
Wouldn't you say?

COCKROACH
Don't fuck it up.

BARD
Chuang Qian Ming Yue Guang.

BOY
"The moonlight upon my rest."

BARD
Yi Shi Dai Tsang Tsang

BOY
"The ground layered with ice."

BARD
Gow Tou Mong Ming Yue

BOY
"Raise your head towards the moon."

BARD
Dai Tow See Gou Huang

BOY
"Lower my head,
Think of home."

COCKROACH
Follow the moon.
Let it remind
Home,
Wherever,
However,
Far you go.

My boy,
You're like me—

BARD
Like us—

COCKROACH
. . . Like us.

You will survive anything.

Now.
Go home.
Put this story to rest.
Sleep.
Perchance to dream.

The end.

acknowledgements

This play was written on the traditional territory of Anishibaabeg, including the Chippewa and the Mississaugas of the Credit First Nation, the Haudenosaunee, and the Wendat peoples.

Infinite gratitude to so many collaborators and artists who made this play possible. Plays come to be through twisty, complex, and often inevitable ways.

This play began as part of Repercussion Theatre's Words with Will commission, entirely as a whole different play named *Whispers*. In 2018 it was graciously workshopped in Montreal with Playwrights' Workshop Montréal with the collaboration of Amanda Kellock, Emma Tibaldo, Jessica Carmichael, Shanti Gonzales, Zina Koro, Alexandre Lavigne, Tsholo Khalema, Kathleen MacLean, Winluck Wong, Li Li, Deena Aziz, and Warona Setshwaelo. This incredible team so gently guided *Whispers* towards the seeds of what *cockroach* came to be, and then that script slept on my laptop, not knowing what to do with it.

With a generous invitation from Joanna Falck in 2019 I was brought in to Tarragon Theatre through two different residency offerings, the Bulmash-Siegel New Creation Development Award and an Ontario Arts Council Playwright Residency, that allowed me to write and explore and grow. That grew to be a commission of some other play, and then COVID hit, and everything was a blur.

Through the murkiness of 2020, Tarragon Theatre proved to be an anchor and a home for continuing any semblance of playwriting. Richard Rose nudged me on, and I went back to *cockroach*, in an attempt to finish it. We workshopped it with incredible actors Augusto Bitter, Kyle Orzech, and Maurice Dean Wint.

When Mike Payette assumed artistic directorship of Tarragon, I was grateful he programmed *cockroach* as part of his first season, and we continued development with collaborators and vital support from Hanna Kiel, Richard Lee, Jeff Yung, Justin Eddy, Myekah Payne, Justin Miller, and Andrea Vagianos.

Then the production, and it was all a dream, everyone on that production team and Tarragon Theatre: Steven, Karl, Anton, Christine, Deanna, Hanna, Mike, Arun, Damon, Myekah, River, Tristan, Emilie, and Jaimee, thank you.

This play took time, and it cost in a way that was very special and, at times, very hard. I am grateful for Pierre for being with me every step of the way. Gratitude to Ian Arnold for seeing this through. Grateful for Brian Quirt, Nina Lee Aquino, and David Yee for endless mentorship. Grateful for Joanna Falck for the faith and her wisdom. Grateful for the Tarragon playwriting community for COVID Zooms. Grateful for organizations who supported with resources and belief: the OAC, TAC, Wuchien Michael Than Fund, the Bulmash-Siegel Foundation, Repercussion, Tarragon, and Playwrights' Workshop Montréal. Thank you to Annie Gibson, Blake Sproule, Avvai Ketheeswaran, Brandon Crone, and Playwrights Canada Press for a beautiful partnership in publication.

I am grateful for audiences at the theatre, and for readers of plays, who gasp, laugh, cry, or sit in confusion, or take naps. You make plays an exciting thing to make, and none of this is possible without you. Thank you.

Jeff Ho (Ho Ka Kei) is a theatre artist, originally from Hong Kong. As an actor, he has toured as Ophelia in Why Not Theatre's *Prince Hamlet* across Canada and the US for over five years. As a playwright, his works include *cockroach (甲甴)*, *Iphigenia and the Furies (On Taurian Land)*, *Antigone: 方*, and *trace*. Jeff is a recipient of the Lambda Literary Award for LGBTQ+ Drama, the Toronto Theatre Critics' Award for Best New Canadian Play, the Jon Kaplan Legacy Fund Award, has been a finalist for the Playwright's Guild of Canada Drama Award and the Governor General's Literary Award, and has been nominated for four Dora Mavor Moore Awards. He is a graduate of the National Theatre School of Canada and currently lives in Toronto.